in the pictu

Joan Chambers and Molly Hood

Acknowledgements

The authors and publishers would like to thank the following children for their special contributions to the artwork in this book: Stuart Carpenter, Benita Chudleigh, Stephanie Ehrlich, Meaghan Gaut, Cassie Huckstepp, Margaret Huckstepp, Jason King, Ellie-May Michael, Brooke Norrie, Pheobe O' Carrigan, Emma Quirk, Tyneille St Quintin, Lâle Teoman-Jeffrey, Amy Vayro.

They would also like to thank the staff and headteacher of Benedict First School, Mitcham, Surrey, for their interest and co-operation during the preparation of this book.

The authors would also like to thank Douglas Chambers for his invaluable assistance.

First published in 1999 by Belair Publications.
Apex Business Centre, Boscombe Road, Dunstable, LU5 4RL.
Email: belair@belair-publications.co.uk

Series editor: Robyn Gordon
Design: Lynn Hooker
Photography: Kelvin Freeman

© 1999 Belair Publications, on behalf of the authors.
Reprinted 2001.

British Library Cataloguing in Publication Data. A catalogue record for this publication is available from the British Library.

ISBN 0 94788 289-8

Contents

INTRODUCTION

In the Picture uses famous paintings as a starting point for introducing a range of themes to stimulate creative learning activities.

- Most of the sections include a colour print of a famous painting, which can be used for discussion in art and language activities.

- Photographs of children's artwork, inspired by these paintings, have been included in each section.

- The selection of famous paintings covers a range of historical periods and artistic styles.

- Information on each painting is given, with a brief reference to the artist. This can be supplemented by the many books currently available.

- Each section includes ideas for a range of ages, which can be adapted if necessary.

- The artwork has been produced using a wide range of media, most of which is easily obtainable. Having a small selection of metallic pens, marker pens and artist's quality pastels available will also be useful. Try experimenting with media other than those specified in the activities to create different interpretations to those suggested. For example, use paint instead of pastels, use lead pencils and charcoals instead of bright colours.

We suggest that the children make a scrapbook about each artist. It could be filled with pieces of their own artwork, postcards, magazine pictures and written information.

The information on the paintings and the instructions for the art ideas, when enlarged or reproduced on an overhead projector, can be used as text for non-fiction study in literacy activities for a large group.

We hope that you will enjoy using this book and find that the paintings are a source of inspiration and creativity.

Joan Chambers and Molly Hood

THE WILTON DIPTYCH, c.1395–99
by Master of the Wilton Diptych

Richard II Presented to the Virgin and Child by his Patron Saint John the Baptist and Saints Edward and Edmund, c.1395–99 (egg on panel) by Master of the Wilton Diptych (fl.c.1395–99) National Gallery, London/ Bridgeman Art Library, London/New York

This work of an unknown artist (possibly French or English) came from Wilton House in Wiltshire, and was bought by the National Gallery, London, in 1929. A diptych is an altarpiece with two panels which fold like a book. This one is made of oak and is small enough to be portable. It has pictures on the outside and inside. The gold leaf was laid on, then polished with agate to make it shine. Small patterns were punched into it with great care so as not to pierce the gold, then the figures were painted on top. Lapis lazuli was used for the deep blue of Mary and the angels.

The left-hand inside panel shows Richard II, King of England from 1377 to 1399, kneeling to pay homage to the Virgin Mary and the Baby Jesus. He is accompanied by St Edmund, holding an arrow to show how he died, St Edward the Confessor, holding the ring he gave to a pilgrim, and John the Baptist, Richard's patron saint.

On the other panel, the angels are all wearing badges showing a white hart (deer) and collars of broomcod (pods of the broom plant). These are the personal emblems of Richard, who is also wearing a broomcod collar. The child is leaning towards him to bless him or to give him the white standard of St George. The angels are in a meadow with flowers, which is in contrast to the plain background in the left-hand panel.

The diptych is believed to have been used by Richard for his own private worship. On the back of the left-hand panel are the Royal Arms of Edward the Confessor (leopards and lilies), but it is damaged. On the back of the right-hand panel is Richard's white hart in a meadow.

SMALL DIPTYCHS
Gold card or card sprayed gold
Dark blue card or paper
Gold pen or paint
Pastels
Scissors and glue

1. Cut out a rectangle of gold card. Fold it lengthways in half.
2. Draw a shape along the top and cut it out, keeping the card folded.
3. Repeat with blue paper or card. Make the blue shape smaller than the gold background by trimming off a small amount around the edge of the whole shape.
4. Glue these two pieces on to the gold card.
5. Using gold pen, draw one figure from the left panel of *The Wilton Diptych* and one angel from the right.
6. Decorate with pastels.

WILTON DIPTYCH REPLICA
Fold a rectangle of gold card in half. Look closely at *The Wilton Diptych* colour plate. Using the blue card or paper, draw the figures from the left in the left panel and from the right in the right panel. Colour with pastel or paint. Cut out and glue down on to the gold card. Cut thin strips of gold card and glue around the edges of both sides of the diptych.

THE WHITE HART

This is a child's version of the picture which is on the back of one of the panels of *The Wilton Diptych*.

Card for background
Gold wrapping paper
Textured wallpaper in a dark colour
Paint in red and dark green
Pastels in pale colours
White card for the animal
Gold pen and small piece of gold paper
Thick black felt-tip pen
Paintbrush and pencil
Scissors and glue

1. Cut a piece of gold wrapping paper large enough to cover the top half of the card. Leave a surplus to fold over at the back.
2. Crush the paper into a ball and open out.
3. Paint over this with red paint. When dry, rub over with a piece of newspaper to give a crazed effect.
4. Cut a piece of wallpaper for the lower half and paint it green. Leave to dry.
5. Glue the gold and green paper on to the background card.
6. Draw and cut out the white hart and glue on to the background. Draw the antlers with gold pen and add features with felt-tip pen. Make a chain and a crown from the gold paper.
7. Use pastels to draw small flowers and leaves.

LARGE DIPTYCHS

Gold card or card covered with gold wrapping paper
Variety of gold papers
White paper for figures
Dark blue paper
Oil pastels
Pencil, scissors and glue

1. Draw a king, queen, angels or nativity scene on the white paper.
2. Colour with pastels. Trace over outline of each figure with a soft pencil. Cut out and glue on to blue or gold paper.
3. Cut round the figure, leaving an edge.
4. Cut out a shape from the gold card. Fold in half symmetrically and glue the figures on each half.
5. Make a frame from contrasting gold paper and glue on to the picture.

- Make a textured frame by spraying corrugated card with gold paint.
- Display on wrapping paper with pictures of angels.

FLYING ANGELS

Dark blue card or paper for
  background and display panels
Gold tissue (wrapping paper) or
  paper sprayed gold
Gold doilies, or white doilies
  sprayed with gold paint
Paper for the angels
Gold pen or paint
Felt-tip pens
Pencil, scissors and glue

1. Draw a side view of an angel
   (without wings) on paper and
   cut it out.
2. Spread glue over the angel
   (apart from the face and
   hands). Place the gold tissue
   paper on this, crumpling it
   slightly as you press down.
   Leave to dry.
3. Decorate the face and hands with felt-tip pens.
4. Turn the angel over and trim off the surplus tissue paper.
5. Make the wings from the gold doily and glue down.
6. Use doily scraps and gold pen to decorate the angel.
7. Mount on dark blue card or paper.

• To make the display panels, cut some rectangles from the background colour. Rule along the edges with
  gold pen. Using gold pen, draw one angel figure from *The Wilton Diptych*. Decorate with pastels.

DOILY ANGEL

Cardboard roll for body of angel
Dark blue paper
Card for face, hands and book
Gold doily
Felt-tip pens
Gold ribbon
Scissors and glue

1. Cut a piece of blue paper
   larger than the cardboard roll.
   Glue the paper on to the roll
   and tuck surplus inside the
   ends.
2. Cut the doily in half and glue
   one half on to the blue paper.
   Trim round this shape to form
   wings.
3. Glue the other half of the doily
   on to the blue roll, making it
   stand out to form a skirt. Glue
   the doily wings on to the back
   of the roll.
4. Cut out a face and hands from
   the card and add details with a
   felt-tip pen. Glue on to the
   body of the angel.
5. Make hair from gold ribbon.
6. Make a small book from card, and glue on to the hands.

ROW OF ANGELS

Rectangle of dark blue paper for background
Gold paper cut into two rectangles the same length, one rectangle half the width of the other
Christmas wrapping paper (blue and gold)
Gold doily
Paper for faces
Felt-tip pens
Pencil, scissors and glue

1. Fold the two gold rectangles together several times concertina-fashion (this makes it easier to fit the wings to the angels).
2. Carefully separate the two rectangles.
3. Refold the wider rectangle, and on to the top layer draw a circle for the head, a triangle for the body and two small rectangles for the arms (joined at the sides).
4. Keeping the paper folded, cut around the shape. Open out the row of angels.
5. On the narrower folded rectangle, on the top layer, draw two wing shapes which are joined together. Cut round these and open out.
6. Place the row of wing shapes underneath the row of angel shapes and glue the angels on to the wings.
7. Cut out haloes from the doily and glue behind the heads.
8. Cut out faces from the paper and glue on to the heads. Complete with felt-tip pens.
9. Glue the row of angels on to the blue background and mount on wrapping paper.

THEME SUGGESTIONS – ANGELS

- Use angels as the basis of a Christmas theme, making a display using Christmas carols, cards and wrapping paper. Add labels to the display to show what the angels are saying, for example *Halleluja*.

- Make a long banner from dark blue paper or thin card. Write the story of 'The Wilton Diptych' in gold pen on the banner.

- Find other paintings of angels (postcards, art books) and try to identify the musical instruments they are playing, for example trumpets and harps. Draw and label where possible.

- Design an angel stencil from card. Look at Christmas cards first. Use this stencil to make a range of Christmas items, for example place mats, serviettes and tree decorations.

- Find pictures of angels on old Christmas cards. Cut them out and glue them on to a piece of blue or gold card. Decorate with Christmas motifs in blue on gold, or gold on blue. Draw your own angel based on this Christmas card angel and photocopy it many times to use as decoration on gifts, cards, etc. Add tinsel and glitter if desired.

- Cut out a large angel shape from gold card. Print rows of Christmas motifs, for example bells, stars and snowflakes, to decorate the angel. These could be made into mobiles by printing on both sides and hanging from a piece of tinsel.

GARDEN OF PARADISE, c.1410
by Master of Oberrheinischer

Garden of Paradise by Master of Oberrheinischer, Stadelsches Kunstinstitut, Frankfurt-am-Main/
Bridgeman Art Library, London/New York

The artist who painted this picture is unknown and is called the Master of the Upper Rhine (Oberrheinischer).
In medieval times, gardens were usually surrounded by walls, both to keep animals and strangers out, and
to create beautiful spaces filled with flowers and fruit.

The carpet of flowers here is similar to the 'Millefleurs' tapestries of the time. Some of the plants shown in
the painting include a cherry tree (called 'the fruit of Paradise'), roses, daisies, purple flag irises, madonna
lilies, lilies of the valley, snowdrops and violets. The garden was a place of peace in which to relax, play
music and games (such as chess and bowls), as well as to grow herbs, vegetables and fruit. Wells,
fountains or fish ponds provided water for the plants and for pleasure.

This medieval garden picture is also a religious painting – showing Mary in blue, reading what is probably the
Book of Wisdom. Mary was known as 'The Mother of Wisdom'. The Christ-child is playing with St Cecilia's
psaltery (she is the patron saint of music). A psaltery is a stringed instrument which was held against the
chest and plucked with both hands. Symbolically, it was associated with gatherings of angels. Many other
things in the garden are symbolic: madonna lily (Mary), food and drink on the table (the Eucharist), water
and song-birds (immortality). St Michael's devil sits at his feet, and St George's dragon lies on its back. The
three figures under the tree provide an amusing contrast to the traditional style of the rest of the painting.

The Paradise garden was thought of in those times as a place of peace and beauty outside this world,
radiant with light, where fruit and flowers never fade. Good Christians imagined they would go there to rest
after this life, to await the Day of Judgement.

MEDIEVAL GARDEN

Blue and green paper for background
Beige or orange paper for wall
White paper for figures, tree, table, etc.
Paint in white, green, blue, red, yellow
   and purple
Cotton buds
Paintbrushes, scissors and glue

1. To make the background, glue green paper for grass on to the blue paper for the sky.
2. Cut out a wall from beige or orange paper and glue it where the above papers join.
3. Draw and cut out those things you have chosen from the Garden of Paradise painting on page 10, for example figures, a table or a tree. Paint them and leave to dry.
4. Glue them down on to the background and print flowers using cotton buds dipped in paint.
5. Mount on gold and red paper. Decorate the red paper using cotton buds and gold paint.

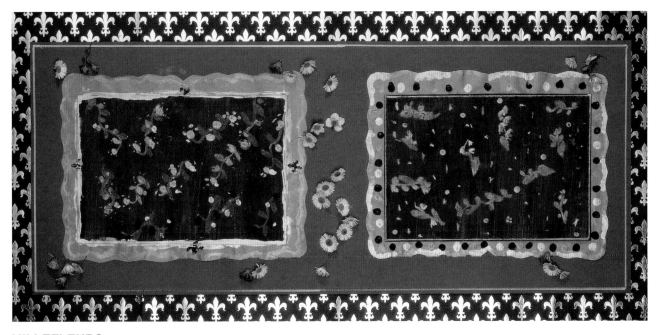

MILLEFLEURS

White paper for background
Pastels
Gold paper or card for frame

Dark green paint
Gold pen or paint
Paintbrushes, scissors and glue

1. Paint the background with the dark green paint and leave to dry.
2. Using a green pastel, draw flower stems all over the background.
3. Draw some small flower-heads along each stem. Use pastels in white, pale blue, yellow and pink.
4. Create an overall design.
5. Glue this on to a piece of gold paper or card which is larger than the picture.
6. Cut around the edge of the gold paper or card in a wavy pattern to create a border.
7. Decorate with gold paint, pens or pastels.

11

LAVENDER DISPLAY

Lavender has been grown in gardens for centuries. In medieval times it had many uses: as a medicine, to promote sleep, to sweeten the air, and as a protection against plague. In more recent times, it has been used to keep clothes fresh and free from moths, and as a perfume in soaps and polishes.

Lavender pictures: Print the stems by using the side of a piece of cardboard and green paint. Make the flower-heads by printing with cotton buds dipped in purple paint.

Lavender sachets: Cut out a section of a doily and glue it on to purple card. Decorate and fill the sachet with real lavender to make a card.

Lavender bottles or sticks:

This is a cardboard version of a real Victorian bottle made of lavender. Cut out a bottle-shaped piece of purple cardboard. Cut long slits into it, almost to the top. Tie a narrow ribbon at one edge at the top and weave it in and out to complete the bottle. Tie off at the end.

IRISES

Place background paper on a wooden surface and rub over with the side of a brown crayon to create a wall effect. Cut out petal shapes for the iris, and glue on to the wall background. Repeat for other flowers. Draw and colour stems and leaves with green crayons.

BIRDS

Draw and cut out leaf shapes and arrange on contrasting background for foliage. Decorate using felt-tip pens and glue down. Draw and colour the birds with crayons or pastels. Cut them out and glue on to the background. Rule a pencil border along each edge of the picture. Decorate the border with small patterns using gold and felt-tip pens. Go over the pencil line border with gold pen.

WALLED GARDEN

Blue paper for background	Scissors and glue
Tissue for plants and flowers	Pastels or chalk
Gold wrapping paper	Felt-tip pens

1. Draw a wall on the blue paper, with space for a statue in the middle.
2. Colour the wall and statue with pastels, chalk or felt-tip pen.
3. Draw trees and plants growing up the wall.
4. Complctc thc picturc and mount it on gold wrapping papcr.
5. Draw and paint a floral border on the mount.

THEME SUGGESTIONS – GARDENS
- Look at the medieval garden in the painting and observe how it is being used, for example for reading, talking, eating, drawing water from the well and picking fruit. Compare with how gardens are used today. Make a miniature book about gardens, with an illuminated letter at the head of each page.

- Visit your local park or public gardens. Photograph all the different aspects, for example flower beds, pathways, steps, water, statues, trees, grass, hedges and walls. Make a display of these with decorated coloured labels.

- Find out about gardens through the ages, for example Roman and Elizabethan. Find drawings and pictures of the period. Use these as inspiration for your own garden design. Make this with collage materials.

SUMMER, 1573
by Giuseppe Arcimboldo (1527– 93)

Summer, 1573 (oil on canvas) by Giuseppe Arcimboldo (1527–93) Louvre, Paris/Peter Willi/Bridgeman Art Library, London/New York

Arcimboldo was the son of a painter who worked in Milan Cathedral. In 1562 he went to Vienna to work at the Hapsburg court and stayed for 25 years as court painter. The Emperor, Maximilian II, commissioned Arcimboldo to paint a Four Seasons series. Arcimboldo painted the Seasons to represent the four stages of adult life: *Spring* as an adolescent, *Summer* as a young man, *Autumn* as a mature man, and *Winter* as an old man.

This portrait consists of different summer fruits and vegetables: the cheek is a peach, the chin a pear, the jacket looks like stalks of corn. The collar has the words 'Giuseppe Arcimboldo F' woven on it (the F stands for 'made' in Latin). The year in which he painted it can be seen at the top of the sleeve.

Maximilian's son, Rudolph II, had a large collection of treasures from around the world, displayed in what were known as 'Rooms of Art and Wonders' – which is where Arcimboldo studied lots of things which he included in his paintings – amazing objects from the ancient past, as well as unusual live animals. His own paintings became 'wonders' like those in the collection.

PROFILE PICTURE

Black paper for background
Beige paper for jacket
Magazine pictures of fruit, vegetables
   and small flowers
Brown wax crayon (wrapper removed)
   and pencil
Green tissue paper strips for the border
Scissors and glue

1. Draw and cut out the jacket.
2. Place this over a textured surface and rub with the side of a crayon. Fringe the collar.
3. Place the jacket on the background.
4. Cut out fruit and vegetables from magazines and arrange to form the profile of a face above the collar.
5. Glue down the jacket and face.
6. Fold the tissue strip over several times. Draw and cut out leaves from the tissue.
7. Glue the leaves and small flowers cut from magazines around the edge to make a border.

FANTASY FACES

Coloured card for
   background
Pictures of fruit and
   vegetables cut from
   magazines, posters
   and wrapping paper.
Felt-tip pens
Scissors and glue

1. Sort the fruit and vegetables into separate groups.
2. Arrange a face, using either fruit or vegetables, on a flat surface.
3. Transfer these pieces on to the background card and glue down.

• Make fantasy animals from left-over pieces. Add details using felt-tip pens.

MAGAZINE PEOPLE
Black paper for background
Pictures of fruit, vegetables and flowers from magazines or wallpaper.
Black marker pen
Scissors and glue

1. Sort the pictures into groups, one of fruit and vegetables and one of flowers.
2. Cut these out and arrange on the background to form a figure.
3. Glue down and decorate with marker pen.

• Instead of using magazine pictures, make fruit, vegetables and flowers from coloured paper. Try arranging them to form other objects, for example, vehicles, buildings and furniture.

FRUIT LADY
• Look at some real fruit and then draw small versions of these in pastel on black paper. Make a figure (male or female) completely from fruit, by copying the small drawings and making them into patterns to form the clothes.

• Younger children will find it easier to draw a pencil outline first and then fill it with fruit patterns.

• Try making a face from fruit patterns. Find a way to make hair, jewellery, etc.

• Make tiny fruits from coloured modelling material. Place these on black card to make faces, figures or animals.

• Arrange real fruit into faces or figures. Photograph or sketch these.

 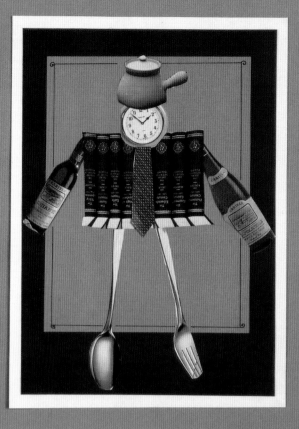

CATALOGUE CUT-OUTS

One of Arcimboldo's most famous paintings was called *The Librarian* (1565). The portrait was made entirely of books.

Cut out pieces from computer magazines and catalogues. Arrange them to form a figure and glue down on to black card. Collect pictures of everyday objects from magazines, catalogues and brochures. Make these into portraits or figures.

THEME SUGGESTIONS – FOOD AND SUMMER

- Look at Arcimboldo's painting. On a coloured piece of paper, draw some of the fruits and vegetables that make the man's face. Label them. Try to find as many as you can. Decorate the edge of the paper with a garland of flowers.

- Write your own name in large double letters. Fill the letters with drawings of fruit and vegetables and colour them with felt-tip pens.

- Discuss the keeping of food, and food hygiene, in the past and the present, for example, preserving and freezing. Make a refrigerator picture with white card and doors that open. Draw or make collage pictures of food and drinks inside. Write a list of the foods you would have for a party.

- The painting of *Summer* on page 14 belongs to a series of the Four Seasons. *Summer* is made entirely of different kinds of fruit and vegetables. The other three paintings in this series are:

  > *Autumn:* a broken tub, a pear, apples, a mushroom, a fig, vine leaves, a pumpkin, and a sweet chestnut.
  > *Winter:* an ancient tree stump with cracked bark, green ivy, a tangle of branches, a straw mat for a cloak, with a coat of arms.
  > *Spring:* petals and stalks of spring flowers, blossoms, a collection of green plants, a lily, a tulip and white flowers.

Draw your own seasonal face using the descriptions above.

WINTER SCENE WITH SKATERS NEAR A CASTLE, c.1608–09
by Hendrik Avercamp (1585–1634)

Winter Scene with Skaters near a Castle, c.1608–09 (oil on panel) by Hendrik Avercamp (1585–1634)
National Gallery, London/Bridgeman Art Library, London/New York

Avercamp was born in Amsterdam but spent most of his life in a very small town called Kampen. He enjoyed watching people involved in winter activities in particular, and made many water-colour sketches to show this. He was deaf and dumb, which may have heightened his awareness of visual detail and explain why he put so much careful detail and close observation into his paintings. These winter scenes look as if they were painted outside on a cold winter's day. In fact, they were painted indoors in a studio, using his coloured sketches.

Although this looks like a real place, it is an imaginary scene. This painting is not very large, but Avercamp has painted everything so clearly, it is possible to see things in the far distance as if looking through a telescope. There are many activities going on: a boy throwing a snowball at a girl, three people sitting in a boat, a man tying a woman's skate, someone at a window, a horse-drawn sleigh moving across the ice and a group of grand people dancing. There are people from all walks of life wearing different types of clothing.

This painting was once a square shape until it was cleaned in 1983. The restorers found that the additions had been added much later, so they were removed and the distinctive circular shape resulted. Avercamp's monogram is at the centre of the lowest part of the painting.

MINIATURE SNOW SCENES

Small circles of beige paper for background
Square of dark brown paper for frame
Black fine-line pen
Coloured pencils
White paint and small paintbrush
Brown wax crayon (wrapper removed)
Scissors and glue

1. Using the fine-line pen, draw on the beige paper a bare tree on the left and a building on the right.
2. Think about the kind of activities that people enjoy in the snow and ice, for example, riding on a sledge, making snowballs, skiing and ice-skating.
3. Draw some of these on the circle.
4. Now draw in the horizon line wherever you wish.
5. Colour lightly with pencils. Using the white paint, add touches of snow on bare branches, roof, etc.
6. For the frame, cut a hole in the centre of the brown paper, slightly smaller than the beige circle.
7. Place the brown frame on a wooden surface and rub firmly with the side of the crayon.
8. Glue the frame on to the beige circle.

- Look at and discuss the activities shown in the painting on page 18.

- Make a list of modern winter activities, for example, skiing, snowboarding, snowmobiling, ski-jumping.

- Make a miniature snow scene in a box (square or round) or on a table-top. Use cotton wool or crumpled white tissue or crêpe paper to make a snowfield. Make people skiing, sledging, etc., from pipe-cleaners and cardboard. Spray artificial snow on the scene. Put clear cellophane across the box or hang in strips above the display table for a wintry look.

- Find a small scene in a magazine and, using white paint, make it into a snow scene by adding snow to branches, rooftops and on the ground.

- Create miniature pictures inside different shaped frames, for example, triangular, rectangular, oval. Notice how the same scene varies within a different shape.

- Make a 'snowstorm' picture by cutting out a ring from silver paper or card. Glue this on to a dark blue background. Draw and cut out figures, mountains and trees from coloured paper and glue down. Using white paint and a narrow brush, make small dabs over the scene to look like snow. While the paint is still wet, add glitter if desired.

WINTER MOBILE

Large cardboard ring
Strips of brown crêpe paper
White cardboard for the background
Cardboard for figures and buildings
Black card for trees
Paints in a variety of colours (similar to those in Avercamp's picture)
Thin paintbrushes
Black marker pen and thin felt-tip pens
Cotton or fishing line for hanging pieces
Gold pen
Pencil, scissors and glue

1. Wrap the strips of crêpe paper around the ring, covering it completely. Glue this down.
2. Cut a semicircle of white card to fit the lower half of the circle.
3. Draw, cut out and paint the figures. Leave to dry. Paint on reverse side too.
4. Outline the figures with a black marker pen and add details with thin felt-tip pens.
5. Decorate some of the clothes with gold pen.
6. Draw and cut out the tree from black card.
7. Draw, cut out and paint the buildings. When dry, outline these and add details with felt-tip pens.
8. Attach cotton or fishing line to all the pieces and hang from the ring.

• Paint and decorate all the mobile pieces on both sides.

• Add other details if desired, for example, a sledge, and a boat.

FOUR SEASONS

Four circles of card or paper for backgrounds in appropriate colours,
   for example green for spring, white for winter
Four semicircles of card or paper in contrasting colours
Black paper or card for frames

Tissue paper
Paints and paintbrushes
Scissors and glue

1. Glue the semicircles on to the circles to create a background for each season. For a more interesting effect, make the colours unusual, for example yellow sky (spring).
2. Draw and paint a picture for each season with a tree on the left and a building on the right. Include suitable activities, for example raking leaves for a bonfire, playing in the snow. Make foreground objects bigger and distant objects smaller.
3. Decorate with tissue paper. Cut out a black frame to fit over the picture.

• These could be made from tissue paper and attached to the window.

THEME SUGGESTIONS – SEASONS

• Look at the clothes people are wearing in the painting, *Winter Scene with Skaters near a Castle.* Some people are wearing rich costumes and others are wearing plain, simple clothes. Make a folder comparing winter clothes of the past and the present.

• Divide the painting in half vertically using string taped at the top and bottom. Each person chooses one half and makes a list of words about that part, for example sledge, boat, castle, tree. Set a time limit, then swap lists. Look at the painting and tick off those things on the list as you find them.

• Write an imaginary story based on a season, for example The Big Freeze. Illustrate this and make it into a zigzag book.

• Decorate four boxes to represent the seasons. Fill each box with pictures and objects which relate to each season. Use these for sorting activities, labelling and guessing games.

THE CHOLMONDELEY SISTERS, 1600–10
Artist unknown

The portrait on the facing page shows two ladies of the Cholmondeley family (pronounced 'Chumley') who came from Cheshire in England. It is one of the oldest paintings in the Tate Gallery, though the artist is unknown. Painters in those days did not always sign their names, but it was probably painted by an artist who lived locally. There is gold writing in the bottom left-hand corner which explains what the picture is about:

> 'Two ladies of the Cholmondeley family
> Who were born the same day
> Married the same day
> And brought to bed the same day.'

The last line means their babies were born the same day. The picture was probably painted to remember these three unusual events and to record the christenings of the babies. At first sight, the ladies look like identical twins, but the writing does not tell us that they were even sisters. They were probably cousins. If you look closely, you can spot differences between them. For example, the lady on the right has brown eyes and the one on the left has blue; the babies do also. The ladies are shown sitting up in bed, wearing grand clothes, with large decorated hoods behind their collars. The babies are in their christening robes which match the patterned fronts of their mothers' dresses. The clothes are painted in great detail and show the importance and wealth of the family. A stiff formality of style was thought important in family portraits to hang in ancestral halls.

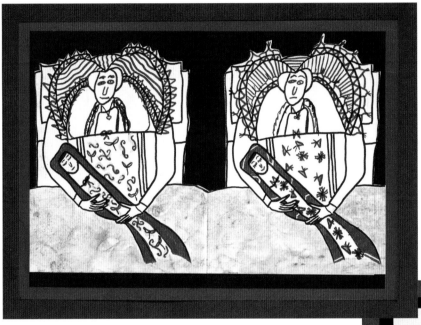

CHOLMONDELEY PORTRAIT
White paper
Fine-line black pen
Red paint or red felt tip pen
Coloured felt-tip pens for details
Scissors and glue

1. Draw the outline of one mother and child with black pen on white paper (keeping the outline as simple as possible).
2. Photocopy this twice and glue these side by side on white paper.
3. Add details with black pen, making one of the mother's clothes match those of her baby. Draw different details on the other mother and child.
4. Colour the shawls and other details.
5. Cut around the two mothers and glue on to black paper.
6. Frame with brown card.

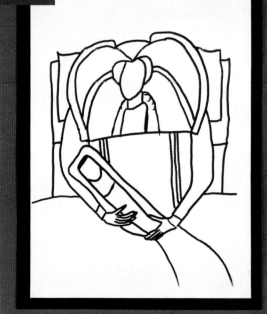

TWENTIETH CENTURY TWINS

Collect mother and baby pictures from magazines, catalogues and cards. Using charcoal, make a sketch of one of the pictures. Photocopy the picture twice and glue these side by side. Using oil pastels or coloured pencils, colour one mother and child so that they have matching clothes. Repeat for the other mother and child. Complete the picture by colouring with pastels.

BABY CARDS

Red card
Silver wrapping paper
Silver pen

Small white doily
Black paper
Scissors and glue

Bootees card

1. Glue silver paper on to the red card.
2. Glue doily on to this.
3. Cut out bootees from silver card. Add red ribbon. Glue on to the doily.

Pram card

1. Glue silver paper on to the front of the card.
2. Cut the doily in half. Glue down and add a quarter of the doily to make a pram.
3. Add wheels and handle cut from black paper.
4. Decorate using the silver pen.

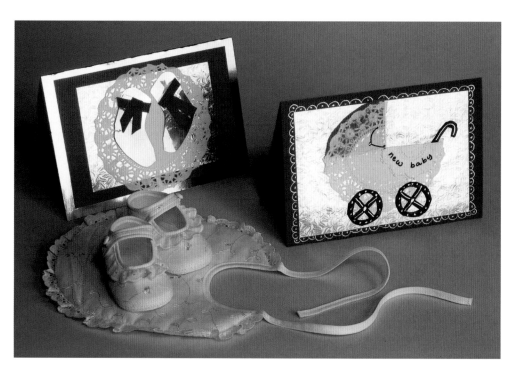

MOTHER AND CHILD

Black paper for mount	Paper in skin tones
White paper	Red paper
Doily	Felt-tip pens
Silver wax crayon (wrapper removed)	Pencil, scissors and glue

1. Place the doily under the white paper and rub over with the side of a silver crayon to make a lacy pattern.
2. Turn the paper over and draw a dress shape. Cut out and glue on to skin-toned paper.
3. Draw a face and hands, etc. Cut these out.
4. Draw a baby shape on the doily pattern and cut this out. Add a face from the same skin-toned paper.
5. Glue mother and baby on to the background.
6. Repeat using the red paper.

• Mount on silver card and add ribbon to make hangers.

THEME SUGGESTIONS – MOTHER AND CHILD

• Bring in a photograph of yourself as a baby with your mother. Make a display of these and compare family likenesses, for example similar eye colour. Guess who each baby is. Write the names under a cardboard flap and check your guess.

• Even though the Cholmondeley sisters aren't twins, they look very similar. Carry out a survey about families which have twins. Make a 'twins' book to include identical and non-identical twins.

• Ask family members about early memories they have of you as a younger child, for example 'What was my favourite baby toy?', 'When did I start to talk and walk?' Make a simple time-line using this information.

• Research traditions for new babies in other countries and cultures, in modern times and in the past, for example swaddling, special gifts and ceremonies. Use a photograph album with adhesive pages to display pictures and information. Decorate the cover.

THE MILLINERY SHOP, 1879–84
by Edgar Degas (1834–1917)

The Millinery Shop, 1879–84, by Edgar Degas (1834–1917), **Art Institute of Chicago/Bridgeman Art Library, London/New York**

Degas was born in Paris – his father a banker and his mother from a wealthy family. He studied law but spent most of his time in the Louvre copying the Old Masters. He painted a range of subjects over and over again including portraits of friends, dancers, laundresses, milliners and jockeys. His subject matter was the modern Parisian life around him. He did not work outdoors as the Impressionists had previously done, but always in his studio. "Art is not a sport," he said.

During the 1880s his failing eyesight caused difficulty for him in the mixing of oils on a palette, so he gradually turned more to pastels which he found easier to use.

In Paris at this time, most millinery shops were exclusive places for wealthy women to visit. The hats were set on stands and placed on a table covered with velvet. Degas prepared for this painting by visiting millinery shops with his women friends while they tried on hats. One friend, Madame Straus, asked what he found most interesting, and he replied, "The red hands of the little girl holding the pins". X-ray photographs of this painting show that he originally painted a rich lady trying on a hat, but he changed it to paint in profile the milliner in her simple dress. She wears a long sewing glove on her right arm and holds a hatpin in her lips, which shows that she makes the hats she sells.

Degas frequently chose an interesting viewpoint from which to paint – for example, in this painting, looking down at an angle. He also shows people and objects (such as hats) cropped by the edge of the painting as they might be in photography, which was a recent invention.

THE HAT SHOP

White card for background
Coloured cardboard for hats and stands
Small pieces of tissue paper in various colours
Orange and green paint
Sponges and brushes
Feathers
Scissors and glue

1. Cut out hat shapes and decorate with small pieces of coloured tissue paper.
2. Cover the background with paint using sponges and brushes. Leave to dry.
3. Cut out one stand for each hat.
4. Arrange the hats and hatstands on the background. Glue down.
5. Glue coloured feathers on to some of the hats.

• Cut out a small piece of velvet and glue on to a smaller piece of card. Fold surplus velvet to the back of the card and glue down. Draw and cut out a single hat shape from coloured paper or card. Decorate as elaborately as possible, using sequins, bows and ribbons, and glue on to the velvet background. Add an elegant price tag, decorate using a gold or silver pen, and display a collection of these small pictures together.

• Make a dressing doll by cutting out a figure from stiff card. Make clothes, uniforms, etc., for the doll from coloured paper or card, with flaps to fold over at the back. Draw and cut out matching hats from card. Cut a slit across each hat which the doll's head will fit into, or use adhesive material to attach the hats.

MINIATURE HATS
Police hat
Cut a strip of black cardboard, and glue the ends together to make a headband. Cut two circles of black tissue paper larger than the headband. Fringe all around the edges and glue on to the headband to make the crown of the hat. Cut out a peak shape from black card and attach to the headband as shown on the opposite page. To make the squared pattern, glue parallel white strips on to black card, leaving spaces in-between. Leave to dry. Cut strips across the striped pattern to give alternating black and white squares. Arrange these strips into a chequered pattern and glue around the hat. Design a police badge.

Tissue-flower hat
Cut out a circle of cardboard for the brim. Cut out a smaller circle in the middle. Cover the brim with two layers of tissue paper on both sides. Cut two circles of tissue paper in contrasting colours, for example yellow and pink. Push the two circles of tissue paper through the hole in the middle with your hand to make the crown. Glue around the edge. Make tissue paper flowers from circles of tissue. Decorate the hat with the flowers and doilies. Add ribbons.

Small circle hat
Cut a small circle from cardboard. Make a large flower from crêpe paper. Cut strips of coloured paper and make into loops. Glue the flower and loops on to the circle and decorate with coloured paper leaves. Add ribbons. Decorate with lace around the edge, if desired.

Peaked cap

Cut a strip for a headband and glue the ends together. Glue a large piece of crêpe paper on to the headband, gather it at the top to form the crown of the hat and glue this in place.

Cut triangles of coloured paper in a contrasting colour and glue them on to the crown. Glue a circle of coloured paper on this to make a button.

Cut out a peak from cardboard and paint it. Make cuts along the straight edge and attach to the headband as shown. Decorate with a badge on the front.

Yellow sun hat

Cut a strip of cardboard to make a headband and glue this together at each end. Place this on a larger piece of cardboard and draw a smaller circle inside the headband. Lift the headband off and draw a larger circle to make the brim. Cut out the smaller circle and make small cuts around this edge (see photograph). Glue this cut edge on to the headband as shown.

Glue a larger circle of yellow tissue paper over the headband to make the crown. Cover the rest of the hat with yellow tissue paper. Decorate with ribbon.

THEME SUGGESTIONS – HATS

- Design and make hatboxes. Set up a hat shop. Label the hats with descriptions and prices. Make and decorate hand written bills. This could be part of an historical display.

- Make two sets of cards, one with pictures of hats, the other with descriptions of who would wear them. Invent your own drama game with the cards.

- To encourage turn-taking during speaking and listening activities, one child in a group chooses a hat to wear. The child wearing the hat is the only person allowed to speak to the group.

- Fill a large bag with a variety of hats, for example sports hat, baby's hat, occupational hat. Use this for a variety of drama and language activities. For example, one child closes his/her eyes and a hat is placed on his/her head. The child asks the rest of the group questions to find out about the hat.

THE LADY OF SHALOTT, 1888
by John William Waterhouse (1849–1917)

The Lady of Shalott, 1888, by John William Waterhouse (1849–1917), © Tate Gallery, London 1999

Waterhouse was born in Rome and lived there until he was six years old. Both his parents were artists. He admired Alfred Lord Tennyson's poetry, and in particular the poem 'The Lady of Shalott' which inspired three of his paintings. He followed the Pre-Raphaelites, who depicted scenes from poetry and mythology. This picture was painted outdoors, possibly in Somerset or Devon, in England. Every detail of the landscape has been closely observed. It shows a moment from the poem:

> *And at the closing of the day*
> *She loosed the chain, and down she lay.*

This painting is now one of the most famous in the Tate Gallery, London.

It tells the story of Elaine, the Lady of Shalott, who was imprisoned in a tower and put under a spell. She was forbidden to look out of the window and was only allowed to see outside through the reflection in the mirror. These scenes were woven into a tapestry on her loom. One day she saw Sir Lancelot in the mirror. She then looked out of the window, breaking the spell. She left the tower and, in a boat, drifted down the river, singing as she died.

> *And as the boat-head wound along*
> *The willowy hills and fields among,*
> *They heard her singing her last song,*
> *The Lady of Shalott.*

Read the poem by Tennyson for the full story.

RIVER SCENE

Large sheet of white paper for background
Strong black paper for the boat
White tissue paper
Small piece of patterned fabric or paper
Thick paintbrushes
Fine black pen
Scissors and glue

Small sheets of white paper for washes
White card or paper for the figure
Paints – green, yellow, blue, black and brown
Small piece of coloured paper for tapestry
Coloured pencils
Gold pen

1. Mix the paints to make a range of blues, greens and browns. Thin these with water and use the blues and greens as a wash to create water on the large sheet of background paper. Leave to dry.
2. Mix several colours for the sky. While still wet, blot with paper for a textured effect.
3. Paint a wash on the smaller sheets of paper in the greens and browns. Leave to dry. Cut into shapes for bushes, trees and foliage.
4. Draw and cut out a boat from black paper and decorate it using the gold pen. (Write 'The Lady of Shalott' along the side of the boat with gold pen.)
5. Draw a figure on the white card and cover it with the white tissue paper. Add features and other details with coloured pencils or fine black pen.
6. Assemble the pieces of the picture and glue on to the background. Make some of these stand out to give a three-dimensional effect.

But Lancelot mused a little space;
He said, 'She has a lovely face,
God in his mercy lend her grace,
The Lady of Shalott.

MEDIEVAL MIRRORS

Draw a circle on white paper. Draw a scene which the Lady of Shalott might have seen reflected in the mirror, for example Sir Lancelot riding past, or the river. Paint with thin brushes and leave to dry. Add details using fine felt-tip pens and decorate using gold pen or paint.

Frame

Make a frame by cutting out a ring from cardboard. Mould pieces of modelling material into shapes and glue on to the ring with strong glue. When dry, paint or spray with silver. Glue the frame on to the painting and trim. Glue jewels or pieces of coloured foil on to the frame.

POETRY SCROLLS

Rule a border around the edge of a piece of beige paper. This beige paper can be made using a thin wash of paint on white paper. Draw a line along the edge with a gold pen. Draw or paint pictures in the border which tell the story of the Lady of Shalott. Colour the border using pastel or paint. Write several verses of the poem on each sheet.

MINIATURE TAPESTRIES

Thread narrow ribbon through a needle which has a large eye. On a square of material which has a large open weave, create a picture or a pattern. Make a loop with ribbon to hang it up, and decorate with a bow.

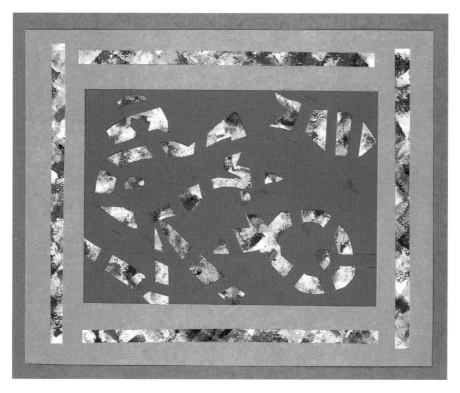

EASY WEAVING

One sheet of green paper for background
One sheet of green paper (same as above) cut into narrow strips
Patterned paper (sponge-printed or wrapping paper)
Larger coloured paper for mounting
Pencil, scissors and glue

1. Draw the outlines of fish on the back of the patterned paper.
2. Cut the centres out of the fish, following the shape of the outline (keep the centres).
3. Glue the fish shapes on to the background. Cut the strips of green paper into smaller pieces and glue these at intervals across the fish outlines. This creates the woven effect when seen from a distance.
4. Decorate with weeds and fish centres. Repeat with the background strips.
5. Glue the picture on to a larger mount and decorate with patterned strips.

• Make sure the narrow strip pieces are long enough to fit across the shapes.

THEME SUGGESTIONS – MYTHS AND LEGENDS

• Read the poem 'The Lady of Shalott' by Alfred Lord Tennyson. This poem contains many images which lend themselves easily to creative artwork, for example:

> Below the starry clusters bright,
> Some bearded meteor, trailing light,
> Moves over still Shalott

The words could be written on a shield shape with gold pen, and displayed with the artwork. Try using Old English lettering.

• Look for one-line images and make a set of miniature pictures to illustrate them, for example *She saw the water lily bloom* or *the mirror cracked from side to side.*

• Read the poem and make a list of unusual words. Make a decorative dictionary with the meanings written beside the words, for example *shallop, gemmy.*

• Make up some language games using the many rhyming words in the poem.

• Create a story corner by decorating a wall to look like a tower. Cut out vines and creepers, to grow up this. Retell stories where someone has been put under a spell or put in a tower, for example Sleeping Beauty, Rapunzel and Rumpelstiltskin.

THE READER, 1896
by Edouard Vuillard (1868–1940)

The Reader, 1896, by Edouard Vuillard (1868–1940), © Photothêque des Musées de la Ville de Paris/P. Pierrain

Vuillard was inspired by the millefleurs tapestries which reminded him of the many patterns that he had been surrounded by all his life, because his mother was a dressmaker and his uncle a textile designer. He liked to paint scenes of everyday life, with people reading or sewing. The greens, pinks and ochres give the look of tapestry to this painting, and the people seem to almost disappear into the patterns.

Vuillard was part of a group called the 'Nabis', from the Hebrew word for prophet - who wanted to move away from Impressionist painting, and towards painting that expressed their spirituality. They emphasised the textures, patterns and expanses of colour for decorative effect.

This painting is one of four panels designed for the library of Vuillard's friend, Dr Vaquiz, in Paris. The panels were in pairs: *The Reader* goes with *The Piano*, and *The Library* with *The Worktable*. They are larger than most of Vuillard's paintings and reflect the activities that would happen in the room for which they were designed.

ROOM IN A BOX

Large cardboard box for the room
Wallpaper (in a variety of patterns with similar colours)
Cardboard for figures and door
Small round box for table
Small rectangular box for settee
Doily
Matchsticks
Felt-tip pens
Scissors and glue

1. Cut out different wallpapers to fit the inner walls of the large box. Glue down.
2. Cover the small boxes with wallpaper and place inside the large box to make furniture. Cover the tabletop with the doily as a tablecloth, and add a small covered bottle top as a vase, with flowers made from matchsticks and wallpaper.
3. Cut out a door from cardboard and glue on to the wall. Draw dresses on the back of the wallpaper and cut these out. Glue each dress on to a larger piece of cardboard. Draw a face, hair and hands with felt-tip pens on the cardboard and cut the figure out. Make the figure stand up by folding the skirt back at the bottom edge.
4. Make cushions from rectangles of wallpaper stuffed with small scraps of paper. Glue the edges together and fringe these when dry.
5. Make rugs by gluing wallpaper on to card and fringing the ends.
6. Make small collage pictures using wallpaper strips as frames, to hang on the walls.

• Use adhesive modelling material to fix the pieces in place, if desired.

• Small groups of children could work together and use this idea to make different rooms, for example kitchen and bathroom. Arrange 'rooms' to create a house or other building. Make people from stiff card or modelling material.

• This three-dimensional idea can be adapted to bring other paintings to life, based on different subjects, for example the forest, the jungle, the sea, animals.

• Create fantasy rooms in, for example a palace, cave or caravan. Make these rooms different shapes.

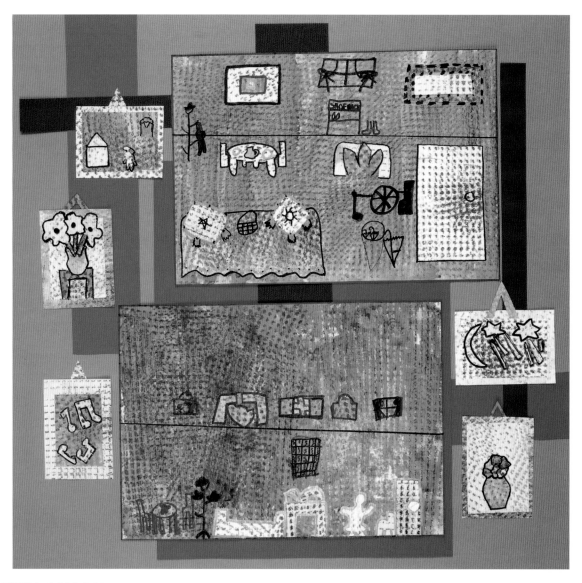

RUBBINGS COLLAGE

White paper for background
Textured surface for rubbing, for example construction toy base plates, wire mesh, etc.
Wax crayons with wrappers removed in shades of, for example, pink, purple, red
Thin paint for wash, for example pink, purple, maroon
Thick paintbrushes for the wash
Felt-tip pens
Scissors and glue

1. Place the paper over the textured surface and rub firmly with the side of a wax crayon.
2. Move the paper round, mixing the colours as required, until the paper is covered. Repeat with several sheets of paper.
3. Using the thick paintbrushes, paint a wash over the crayon pattern. Leave to dry.
4. When dry, choose one sheet as a background for a room and cut up the other sheets of paper to make windows, doors, furniture, etc.
5. Glue these on to the background and decorate with felt-tip pens.

• Use left-over pieces of paper to make small pictures with frames.

• Make four panels linked by a common theme for other rooms in the house, for example kitchen or bedroom. Make an identical pattern along the top of each as Vuillard did in his series.

• Find some material scraps with small patterns on them. Using strong glue, make a picture by cutting out the shapes and patterns and gluing them on to a larger piece of patterned material.

BOOKMARKS

Cardboard for bookmark
Large motifs cut from wallpaper
Chalks or pastels in colours to match
  motifs
Pieces of fringe
Scissors and glue

1. Glue the motifs on to the cardboard.
2. Use chalks or pastels in matching
   colours to continue the shapes of the
   motifs and fill in the spaces.
3. Spray with fixative, or cover with
   adhesive plastic.
4. Glue a small piece of fringe at one
   end.

THEME SUGGESTIONS – HOMES

- Make the picture in a box (see page 35), and write a script about what is happening. Who are the people? Write about their conversation. Record it on a tape recorder.

- Use the picture in a box for an instructional drawing game. One child describes the scene in the box and the rest of the group turn their backs to the box and draw it from the instruction. Compare the results and see which picture suits the description best.

- Design a patchwork cushion using six patterns from your own house, for example curtains, settees and wallpaper patterns.

- Collect scraps of fabric with small patterns. Cut a hole in each piece of fabric and glue it on to a white background. Colour in the hole with the same pattern.

- On small cards, draw and label objects from your home, for example table, lamp, chair. (one set for each room). Make another matching set to play Snap, or a memory game.

THE WHITE HORSE, 1898
by Paul Gauguin (1848–1903)

The White Horse, 1898 by Paul Gauguin (1848–1903) Musée d'Orsay, Paris/Giraudon/Bridgeman Art Library, London/New York

Paul Gauguin was born in Paris and, as a young baby, sailed with his family to Peru in South America. He lived there till he was six, and loved the sunlight, heat and the brightly coloured, scented plants. Later, he joined the Navy and sailed round the world before becoming a businessman in France. Gauguin was a self-taught painter and learnt about art through buying and collecting paintings by artists of the time, such as Monet and Degas. He became friends with Van Gogh, and they often painted together. They were known as Post Impressionists.

This picture was painted on his second trip to Tahiti, where he lived for several years. It was a sad time in his life, as he was poor and very ill. He painted this picture when he began to feel better. It was painted on a roughly textured canvas using strong brushstrokes and a palette knife. This helps to create a mysterious and wild effect. He was inspired by the horse sculptures of the Parthenon, and his childhood rocking horse. The horse in the foreground is not white but greenish-grey because of the reflection of the leaves protecting it from the sun. Gauguin was influenced by Japanese art, and this shows in the way the tree branches go diagonally across the painting to help divide the background.

FOREST SCENE

White paper for background	Crêpe and tissue paper in blue, white and a variety of greens
White card for horses	Pale blue tissue paper larger than the white background paper
Small scraps of fabric	Coloured squares of paper in shades of green
Paintbrushes	Paints in white, green, yellow and brown
Pencil, scissors and glue	Small box or piece of cardboard roll (to make the horse stand out)

1. Cover the white paper with the pale blue tissue, and glue the surplus on to the back.
2. Look at the background colours of Gauguin's painting and cut and glue flat pieces of tissue paper for the water and other background areas.
3. Cut crêpe paper into strips and crunch or twist on to the background. Add the other materials to create the textured background.
4. Draw and cut out two horses, one smaller than the other.
5. Paint the larger horse white and pale green and the smaller one brown. Leave to dry.
6. Glue the white horse on to the small box, and then glue this and the smaller horse on to the background.
7. Dab the background with paint.

TISSUE PAPER ABSTRACT
White paper for background
Tissue paper in blue, green, red and purple
White paper for horse
Black or blue felt-tip pen
Scissors and glue

1. Tear the tissue paper into pieces.
2. Spread glue on the upper part of the white background paper and press some of the tissue pieces on to it. Make these overlap.
3. Repeat on the lower part of the paper.
4. To give a neat edge, fold the surplus tissue paper on to the back and glue down.
5. Look at Gauguin's painting and draw some of the features, for example leaves, rocks, flowers, plants and trees, on top of the tissue paper.
6. Draw and cut out a white horse. Glue the horse on to the picture.

• Make the mount by covering a larger piece of paper with tissue paper. Fold the surplus on to the back and glue down. Glue the horse picture on to the mount.

• Make a horse from white modelling material or clay. Make a tropical background in a box. Stand the horse in the box.

• Make a Tahitian corner for displaying artwork. Tear large pieces of tissue paper into abstract shapes to make a tropical forest scene by hanging them down from fishing line. Drape brightly coloured material across the back and over the table. Make flowers from white or coloured tissue paper, or use real flowers and arrange them in the scene. Add tropical fruits, for example mangoes, melons and bananas, in wooden dishes or baskets.

MAGAZINE ANIMALS

Coloured card for background
Thin paints or coloured inks
Pieces of sponge

Picture of an animal cut from a magazine
Paintbrush
Scissors and glue

1. Colour the picture of the animal using paint or ink.
2. Create a fantasy background by dabbing with pieces of sponge dipped in paint or ink. If desired, details can be added with felt-tip pens.
3. Glue the animal on to the background card.

THEME SUGGESTIONS – ANIMALS

- Inside a large horseshoe shape, draw objects associated with horses, for example stable, hay, saddle. Label these. Draw a grid with different headings, for example food, home, work, sport. Refer to the horseshoe shape and sort the labels in the correct columns.

- Look at Gauguin's *The White Horse*. In Tahitian culture, this was a sacred animal. Write a story about a horse with magical powers who drinks from a pool and has adventures on a tropical island. Display on a colourful tropical background.

- Make horse head puppets on sticks. Try this with other animals. Write a play script for the puppets.

- Find out about the use of horses in the past and present, for example ploughing, pulling carts, canal boats, delivering mail. Make posters on coloured paper for 'Then and Now', for example *horse and cart – car*.

CHARING CROSS BRIDGE, LONDON, 1906
by André Derain (1880–1954)

Charing Cross Bridge, London, **John Hay Whitney Collection © 1999**
Board of Trustees, National Gallery of Art, Washington, 1906, canvas

André Derain was born in Chatou, a suburb of Paris. His father sold dairy products and was also a member of the local council. Derain's parents hoped he would become an officer or an engineer, but he wanted to be a painter. At first he studied with a local artist, painting scenes of the Chatou area before going on to art college. As well as painting, he was interested in reading, and produced many illustrations for newspapers and books. He even wrote a novel of his own. In the meantime, he had become friends with Matisse and a group of young painters, including Dufy. They put on an exhibition in Paris in 1905. These pictures in strong colours and bold, powerful brushstrokes caused an outcry amongst the viewers and the newspapers.

The group became known as 'Fauves' or 'wild beasts'. Their subject matter was really colour itself – expanses of paint straight from the tube - primary colours contrasting with their opposite colours to create a vibrant effect. Even a winter's day in London could be seen as exotic and filled with light by exaggerating the colours of the actual scene.

Derain spent two months in London in the winter of 1906 and produced many paintings and drawings of local scenes. This view was painted from the south bank of the Thames, standing on the wharf near Lion's Brewery, a well-known building at the time, which is the blue building on the left side. He also had a view of the bridge with the train moving across it into the station. The water is painted with short, rough brushstrokes, but the Houses of Parliament in the distance and the other buildings are more smoothly painted.

CRÊPE PAPER CITYSCAPE

Paper for background
Crêpe paper in red, blue, yellow, orange, purple and green
Small piece of card for the train
Thick paint in some of the above colours
Paintbrushes
Cardboard rolls or small boxes for the bridge
Scissors and glue

1. Fold the paper to make the edge of the river.
2. Spread glue over the area above the line. Place a large piece of crêpe paper over it. Create a crinkled effect by crushing the paper on to the glue.
3. Repeat with smaller pieces of crêpe below the line for the river.
4. Draw and cut out a building skyline from crêpe. Glue on to the background.
5. Cover cardboard rolls or boxes with crêpe paper and glue across the river to create a bridge.
6. Draw and cut out a small train. Glue it on to the bridge.
7. Complete the picture by adding contrasting dabs of paint.

• Make a three-dimensional display using boxes and cardboard rolls covered with crêpe paper. Create a scene based on water and a bridge. Use the three primary colours and the three secondary colours, putting the complementary pairs together, for example purple and yellow. Crumple and crush crêpe paper to achieve a three-dimensional effect for the river. Use the colours that Derain used in his painting of Charing Cross Bridge. When the picture is dry, paint with dabs of contrasting colours.

RIVERSIDE

Two sheets of coloured paper of the same size, in contrasting colours
Oil pastels in red, yellow, blue, green, orange and purple only
Small strips of card for the bridge and train

1. Fold one of the coloured papers at an angle.
2. Draw a row of buildings along this fold with different roof shapes and heights. Colour solidly with pastels and add some details.
3. Cut out along the roofline of the buildings and glue this picture on to the other coloured paper to create the sky.
4. Make the river by drawing with pastels in small horizontal blocks of colour. Draw the boats on the river.
5. Colour one strip to create the bridge and glue this across the river at both ends to make it three-dimensional.
6. Draw a train on the other strip of card, cut out and glue it on the bridge.

• Find another painting with a river in it, preferably one that looks realistic. Make a 'Fauve' version of the picture, using primary and secondary colours in paint, pastel or crayon.

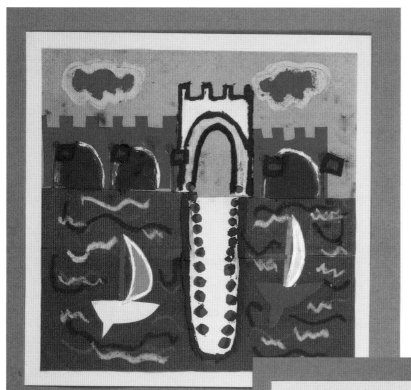

These pictures are made using only red, blue, green and yellow. Make a picture which has a bridge, a river, buildings and some boats.

IMAGINARY SCENE

Square of coloured paper for the
　background in red, blue, green or
　yellow
Paper in the remaining three colours
Pastels, felt-tip pens or paints in the
　same colours
Scissors and glue

1. Set out paper in the four colours.
　Choose one for a background.
2. Draw and cut out the boats,
　buildings and landscape, and glue
　on to the background.
3. Add details using pastels, felt-tip
　pens or paints.

• Use the same technique for portraits or still-life pictures.

• Draw an outline of a boat or bridge with felt-tip pen. Colour it in using the three primary and three secondary colours. Cut around the edge of the shape and glue it on to a plain colour or black.

• Cut out purple, green and orange boats. Make flags for them in their complementary colours. Glue them on to a plain piece of paper. Colour the paper with all six colours in wavy shapes to represent water.

• Bring in some toy boats. Create a river scene using construction toys. Use different coloured materials to make the river.

BLUE BRIDGE

White paper for background
Red, yellow and green paint
Blue paper for bridge
Blue marker pen
Pieces of sponge or sponge brushes
Scissors and glue

1. Sponge the white paper background with red, yellow and green paint. Leave to dry.
2. Draw and cut out a bridge from the blue paper. Glue on to the background.
3. Complete the picture by adding details of buildings, roads, cars, boats, etc., using blue marker pen.

• Find pictures of famous bridges, for example Tower Bridge in London, England; Sydney Harbour Bridge in Australia; the Golden Gate Bridge in San Francisco, USA; the Forth Bridge in Scotland, and the Ponte Vecchio in Florence, Italy. Display these pictures around a map of the world. Use narrow coloured ribbons and pins with coloured heads to connect the country to the picture. Find out the correct names for each type of bridge, for example suspension, arch, bascule, and make labels under the pictures.

• Collect postcards of bridges and display these in the shape of a bridge on a brightly coloured background.

• Collect postcards of bridges, read the information on the back and then put them in order of building date in a scrapbook or an old photograph album. Copy the information from the back of the postcards on to coloured labels.

• Construct a three-dimensional bridge from junk or construction materials and find ways to make it open and close for river traffic.

PANORAMIC PICTURE

This is a group activity for three people. Each child has one piece of paper, which is passed on to another person when each part is complete.

Rectangular piece of white paper (divided approximately in three with soft pencil line, drawn vertically)
Pastels
Fine-line black pen

1. Using the black pen, draw a river across the white paper background.
2. The first person draws a city scene on the first one-third of the paper. It can be realistic or fantasy. Colour it with pastels and, when complete, pass it on to the next person.
3. The second person continues the picture on the next third of the page (continuing the lines for roads or paths).
4. The third person finishes the picture.

- Try to include different parts of a city, for example an airport, bus station, town centre or park.
- Explain and describe each third of the picture when it is passed on to the next person.

THEME SUGGESTIONS – CITIES

- Find paintings of rivers. Write about some of the activities connected with the rivers, for example Constable's *The Hay Wain* – noting the horses, cart, people, etc.

- Discuss and write about ways to cross water in modern times. Compare these with those of the past. Make a book called 'Water Crossings' – past, present and future.

- Find a river near you. Research its history and the people who lived and worked near it. For example: What buildings are near the river? How old are the buildings? What are their uses?

- Find out about places for children to visit in cities, for example, museums, adventure playgrounds, bowling alleys, swimming pools, parks, football pitches. Mark these on a city map with three-dimensional flag labels.

- Make a graph of favourite out-of-school activities. Discuss ways to improve city life for children. Which activities would you like to try (for example, ice-skating and indoor football)?

- Discuss ways of using rivers and waterways in the future to transport people and goods. Design a rivercraft for this.

SWINGING, 1925
by Wassily Kandinsky (1866–1944)

Swinging, 1925, by Wassily Kandinsky (1866–1944), © Tate Gallery, London 1999 © ADAGP, Paris and DACS, London, 1999

Kandinsky was born in Moscow in Russia. He studied Law and Politics at Moscow University and later became a teacher of Law. One day, Kandinsky went to see an exhibition of French Impressionist paintings. It changed his life. He was so moved and impressed by the paintings that he decided to leave his successful job and move to Munich in Germany to study art. Later he travelled to Italy, Holland and Tunis, and eventually put on an exhibition of his pictures in Paris.

He became known as one of the best early painters of abstract art. Kandinsky was called an Expressionist painter because he expressed his feelings and ideas through the use of line, shape, colour and symbols. He taught at a famous school of modern design in Germany and wrote books about the theory of art. One of his theories was that certain shapes give certain colours more impact. To test this, he gave his students a triangle, circle and square to colour in red, blue and yellow using one colour on each shape. Most students coloured the triangle yellow, the circle blue and the square red. He then used other shapes and the colours green, orange and purple. The original German title of this painting was *Schaukeln* and has sometimes been translated as 'shaking' or 'rocking'. It was thought that *'Swinging'* was the best English translation. Kandinsky prepared for his paintings with many drawings and watercolours, but there appears to be none for this painting.

ABSTRACT COLLAGE

Sheets of coloured card in green, blue and yellow
Paint in bright colours, plus white
Oil pastels

Black paper or card (for some of the shapes)
Pieces of sponge
Scissors and glue

1. Choose one of the sheets of coloured card for the background, for example green.
2. Sponge-print over this with yellow, green and white paint. Leave to dry.
3. Sponge-print other sheets of card in contrasting bright colours, for example purple, orange, dark green. Leave to dry. Cut into shapes and decorate them with left-over scraps and black paper or card.
4. Arrange the shapes on the background, then glue these down.
5. Decorate with pastels.

• This can be a group activity where the sponge-printed card can be shared to produce a greater variety of colours.

• Make mobiles from cardboard using some of the interesting shapes in *Swinging*. Cut them out and staple them on to a large cardboard shape, for example triangle, square, circle, etc. Hang them from fishing line.

• Using the sponge-printing technique, make large shape pictures. Glue a small shape, for example a triangle, on to a larger shape, for example a square, then on to an even larger shape, for example a circle. Overlap these to make a large abstract picture.

SWINGING SHAPES

Large sheet of coloured card for background
Sheets of newspaper
Sheet of coloured card for three-dimensional pieces
Pieces of thin polystyrene
Paint in bright colours
Paintbrushes
Coloured string or narrow ribbon
Small cardboard boxes for three-dimensional shapes
A variety of simple plastic shapes in different sizes to use as templates, for example square, circle.
Pencil, scissors and glue

1. Draw and cut out shapes from the polystyrene using the templates.
2. Spread paint thickly over one side of a polystyrene shape and press on to newspaper to remove any surplus.
3. Place this shape on the coloured card background and press carefully along the edges. Remove carefully and reprint several times across the background until the paint runs out.
4. Repeat with the other shapes and paints, overlapping the prints.
5. Print some separate shapes on to the other sheet of card. When dry, cut these out.
6. Tape string or ribbon on to the back of each printed shape. Tape the other end of the string to the back of the matching painted polystyrene printing block.
7. Glue a small box on to the back of each printed shape and glue to the background so that the polystyrene shapes hang down.

CONNECTING SHAPES

Blue card for background
Pieces of card in other bright colours, plus black
Scissors and glue

Picture

1. To make flat pictures, cut shapes, for example a triangle, square or circle, from the coloured and black card.
2. Cut a slit in each shape and fit them together. Try various patterns before gluing them down on to the background.

Sculpture

1. To make the free-standing shape, cut slits in two squares of card to form a base. Fit them together.
2. Cut out other shapes from card. Cut a slit in each and fit them together to make a sculpture.

THEME SUGGESTIONS – COLOUR, SHAPE AND PATTERN

- Draw a large geometric shape and, inside it, write and draw five things you think you can see in *Swinging* (for example, traffic lights, the moon, etc.).

- Look at *Swinging* and write an account of what you think is happening. Rewrite it in coloured felt-tip pens, making the words look more interesting by stretching, curving, twisting and moving the letters in different directions across the page.

- Make a swing from cardboard and scrap materials. Cut out a figure using some of the shapes in the painting and place on the swing. Suspend the swing from a line and make it move. This could be used as part of a circus theme.

- Copy some of the shapes, label them and transform them into something else, for example circle – balloon; semicircle – umbrella.

POPPIES, c.1927
by Georgia O'Keeffe (1887–1986)

Poppies (oil on canvas) by Georgia O'Keeffe (1887–1986), Private Collection/Christie's Images/
Bridgeman Art Library, London/New York © ARS, NY and DACS, London 1999

Georgia O'Keeffe grew up on a farm in Wisconsin, USA, between the great forests and the open prairies, where she loved exploring the countryside in different seasons. She said that autumn was her favourite season.

She went to art school where she painted to music, creating beautiful abstract shapes in works such as *Music Pink and Blue*. Later she moved to New York, where she saw exhibitions of modern European paintings. She married Arthur Stieglitz, whose close-up photographs inspired her to look at ordinary things (buildings, flowers, clouds) in a different way. She painted many common flowers – poppies, irises, roses, lilies – so closely that they fill the canvas. She said, "I'll paint what I see, what the flower is to me, but I'll paint it big and they'll be surprised into taking time to look at it."

She used a very fine canvas and special primer to make a perfectly smooth surface for painting the petals and leaves of the flowers. She had a great love of the plant world. Once she refused to see a visitor in case the flower wilted before she had finished painting it. She was interested in the shapes and colours that emerged when she took time to examine the flowers in extreme close-up.

In her long life, she explored all sorts of other themes, including clouds, skulls, lakes, skyscrapers, rocks, hills and deserts.

POPPY PICTURES

These were inspired by one of Georgia O'Keefe's paintings of Oriental poppies.

White paper for background
White paper for flowers, same size as above
Thick paint in red, orange and black
Large paintbrushes
Pencil, scissors and glue

1. Paint the white paper background red and add touches of orange. Leave to dry.
2. Draw large poppies on the other sheet of white paper. Cut them out and paint orange. Add touches of red. Paint the centres black. Leave to dry.
3. Glue the poppies on to the painted background.

PAPER POPPIES

Tissue paper in red, orange and black
Plant sticks or strong plastic straws
Strips of green crêpe paper for stem
Masking tape
Pencil and card
Scissors and glue

1. To make the stem, fasten the crêpe paper to the bottom of the stick with tape.
2. Cover the stick by twisting the crêpe paper along it. Fasten at the top with tape.
3. Make a template of a petal by drawing a round shape on card. Cut this out.
4. Place the template on top of three layers of red and orange tissue and draw around it. Cut through the three layers. Repeat several times.
5. Crush black tissue and place on a black tissue paper circle. Push the stem into this, gather the crushed paper inside the tissue paper circle and fasten with tape to the stem to form a black ball as the centre of the flower. Add fringed black strip if desired.
6. Place one petal shape on top of another and gather both together with tape on to the stem around the black centre. Continue this process to make a large poppy head. Cover any tape that shows with green crêpe paper.

GIANT FLOWERS

White card cut in a large circle
Roll of white crêpe paper (cut in wide strips
  while paper is still folded – see illustration)
Small circle of black tissue paper
Paint in pale pastel colours
Felt-tip pens and paintbrushes
Scissors and glue

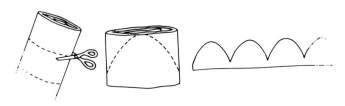

1. To make the flower on the right, cut out a scallop shape from one edge of the folded crêpe strip. Open it out to create a long strip of petals (see illustration above).
2. Gently stretch the edge of each petal.
3. Spread glue around the edge of the circle of card.
4. Start at the outer edge of the card circle and gently press unstretched edge of crêpe paper into the glue. Follow the shape of the circle.
5. Spread glue over the rest of the circle.
6. Continue pushing crêpe paper into the glue, overlapping and gluing until the centre of the flower is complete.
7. Glue the black tissue circle into the centre of the flower.
8. Dab petals with paint.

- Repeat the strip technique for other large petal-shaped flowers. Make a large trumpet for the centre by wrapping a strip of crêpe paper around your hand and twisting it at the base. Spread glue in the centre of the flower and press the trumpet on to it. Apply glue stick around the edge of the trumpet and dab it into powder paint. (See the flower on the left of the photograph.)

- If desired, cut out a small figure from card. Decorate with white crêpe paper and felt-tip pens. Imagine this figure lives inside the flower, and write a story about it.

- Look at the instructions for three-dimensional poppies (on page 53). Make a giant flower using this technique from a variety of pastel coloured tissue papers. Attach to a long stick covered with tissue paper, and add coloured streamers to the stem if desired. Use for stage decoration or stage performances.

- Create a hanging garden using flower heads made as above. Hang at different heights using green ribbon or plaited strips of green crêpe paper.

LINE FLOWERS

White paper for
   background
Coloured felt-tip
   pens
Pastels (not oil),
   or chalk

1. Draw some small flower shapes at random on the white paper background.
2. Increase the size of each flower by following the shape with a continuous line around the flower.
3. Where the flowers meet, continue the line under or over each shape.
4. Colour with pastel or chalk and blend the colours by gently rubbing.

• Explore ways of enlarging flowers from photographs or pictures by, for example, photocopying, using a magnifying glass or a simple grid.

MINIATURE FLOWERS

Find a very tiny flower. Look at it under a magnifying glass. Select paper the same colour as the flower. Draw and cut out the flower head. Glue on to a small coloured piece of paper and decorate with pastels.

WHITE FLOWERS (JIMSON WEEDS)

One of Georgia O'Keeffe's famous paintings was of the Jimson Weed
  (see photographs of this plant in the display below).

Blue paper for background
White tissue paper
Felt-tip pens and pastels (not oil) in pale colours
Scissors and glue

1. Place three pieces of tissue paper on top of each
   other. Draw a flower shape on the top layer.
2. Hold the three layers of tissue together and cut
   out the shape.
3. Glue each layer in the centre.
4. Spread a little glue on the blue background paper
   and press the flower on to it.
5. Decorate with felt-tip pens and pastels.

• To make the other flowers in the display, look at the
  photographs of the Jimson Weed. Draw the flower
  outline on white paper. Place this on top of several
  pieces of white paper. Hold the layers together and
  cut the flower shape to produce identical flowers.
  Decorate with pastels. Use as a background to
  display the children's work.

FELT FLOWERS
Cut white felt into a variety of flower shapes, and decorate with pale coloured pastels. Arrange the flowers on to a contrasting felt background. Glue down if desired.

THEME SUGGESTIONS – FLOWERS
- Classify flowers by colour. Make lists on appropriately coloured paper, for example yellow: daffodil, dandelion, sunflowers.

- Make a list of people's names which are those of flowers, for example Rose, Daisy, Pansy, Hyacinth, Lily, Violet, Petunia, Iris. Draw a figure to illustrate each name, and decorate with appropriate colours. Make a miniature book about each flower.

- Look at flower and plant emblems used by different countries, for example thistle for Scotland, wattle for Australia, edelweiss for Switzerland. Match the flags of the countries with their flower emblem. Make into a display.

- The Victorians decorated their Christmas cards with many flowers and plants which are not seen on modern cards, for example ivy, pansies, roses, violets. Design a modern Christmas card with flowers.

- Collect a variety of flowers and sort them according to the number of petals. Place them in small decorated pots and write the relevant number of petals on each pot.

- Grow a flower in a pot. Photograph it at different stages of growth and make a display.

- Cut out pictures of flowers from magazines. Draw a flower shape with a stem on a rectangular piece of card and cover the flower shape with cut-out flowers in one colour. Use this as a bookmark.

REGATTA AT COWES, 1934
by Raoul Dufy (1877–1953)

Regatta at Cowes, **Ailsa Mellon Bruce Collection, © 1999 Board of Trustees, National Gallery of Art, Washington, 1934, oil on linen**

Raoul Dufy was born in Le Havre, a town in Normandy, France. He grew up in an ordinary family with five sisters and three brothers. Le Havre was a busy port and Dufy loved watching the different types of boats coming and going, especially the old sailing ships.

When he was fifteen he became interested in art and went to evening classes in Le Havre. Later he went on to study art and got to know the painters Matisse and Derain. He was very much influenced by Matisse's paintings and, for a while, was one of the group known as 'Fauves'. Dufy was very versatile. As well as being a painter, he was known as a brilliant fabric designer. He also designed stage sets, tapestries, furniture, menus and posters.

He was a happy, optimistic person who loved life. Dufy particularly liked going to events where there were lots of people enjoying themselves. He painted horse races in England, harvests in Normandy, jazz bands in Mexico, regattas in France and England, as well as gala evenings, concerts and sporting activities.

Dufy particularly loved regattas, probably because of his childhood interest in boats. The one shown in the picture takes place annually in Cowes, on the Isle of Wight, which is off the south coast of England. This painting shows the pleasure he had in the streamers, flags and bustle. The oil colours are spread lightly and freely, in thin strokes like a watercolour sketch. The joyful atmosphere he creates in his pictures made him a very popular painter.

SAILING BOATS

Small sheet of white paper
Wax crayons in bright colours
Wax crayons in blues and greens
   (for water)
Scissors or blunt pencil

1. Draw the outlines of boats and flags
   with the brightly coloured wax
   crayons, pressing firmly.
2. Fill these shapes with colours which
   contrast with the colours of the lines.
   (Try not to leave any white spaces.)
3. Colour all the spaces between the
   boats and flags with the blue and
   green wax crayons.
4. Using contrasting colours, add
   another layer of crayon to parts of
   the picture. Press firmly.
5. Using scissors or a blunt pencil,
   scratch patterns and lines into the
   double layers of wax to reveal the
   colour underneath.

• For a better effect, use lighter colours
  underneath.

• Use this technique on a sheet of
  paper, then cut it into strips to make a
  picture frame.

TISSUE BOAT SCENE

Coloured paper for background
Blue tissue paper larger than background
Pieces of thin card and coloured tissue paper (not blue)
Pieces of sponge
Paint in pale colours
Felt-tip pens
Scissors and glue

1. Spread glue over the background paper.
2. Press the blue tissue paper on to this.
3. Fold the surplus tissue paper on to the back and glue down.
4. Cut out a boat and two separate sails from the pieces of thin
   card. Cover each piece with different coloured tissue paper.
   Glue on to the background.
5. Sponge-print flags on to the blue tissue paper and decorate
   with felt-tip pens.

• Collect postcards and magazine pictures of boats and make a
  montage on a large background of blue card. Create your
  own small flag design with coloured paper, and use the flags
  to make a decorative border.

59

WATER-LINE

White and coloured card
Collage materials, for example sequins, scraps of ribbon, braid, glitter, coloured paper and shiny paper
Coloured felt-tip pens (not black)
Strips of crêpe paper, shiny paper and thin cardboard in white and shades of blue (for water effect)
Scissors and glue

1. Fold a piece of coloured card in half. Draw and cut out the base of the boat, starting at the fold, which is the top of the boat (keeping the card folded).
2. To make the sails, fold another piece of card in half. Draw a line starting at the fold to form a triangle. Keep the card folded and cut along the line.
3. Glue the folded sail on to the boat.
4. Make flags from small pieces of card, and decorate. Glue on to the sails.
5. Decorate the boats with collage material.
6. Draw and cut out underwater creatures from card, for example fish, octopus, starfish and sharks.
7. Decorate with collage materials.
8. Make paper chains from blue and green paper and attach to fish, etc.
9. Hang these from a wire or cotton line. Add zigzag strips of crêpe paper, cardboard and shiny paper spirals.
10. Sit the boats on the line.

• This could be made into a river scene. Place folded ducks, swans, etc., on the line which represents the river.

• Use the line idea to represent other themes, for example above the ground, or under the ground. Place the line in front of a coloured paper background, blue for the sky and brown for underground. Place plants, trees, etc., on the line, showing root systems below.

FELT PICTURES
Blue felt for background
Pieces of felt in bright colours, for example red, yellow and green, plus white
Pastels
Scissors and strong glue

1. Cut out sailing boats from the pieces of felt. Arrange the boats on the felt background before gluing down.
2. Cut out flag shapes from felt. Decorate with pastels and smaller pieces of felt.
3. Draw wave patterns with pastels on the felt background. Try adding some boat reflections.

• If felt is not available, use a large sheet of white paper. Cut a cardboard strip into wave shapes and place under the paper. Rub over with the side of a wax crayon (using blues and greens). Move the strip around and rub firmly to create a water effect. Wash over with thin blue and green paint. Leave to dry. Cut boats and flags from coloured paper and glue on to the background. Decorate with felt-tip pens.

THEME SUGGESTIONS – WATER
• Cut out pictures associated with water from magazines and travel brochures. Make a scrapbook of these to show a variety of water sports and activities.

• Make a boat race game on a large sheet of coloured card. Make three-dimensional boats from modelling material and paper sails.

• Find out about regattas and famous boat races around the world. Find out where they take place and mark these with flags on a large map showing the relevant information.

• Keep an imaginary log of a long sea journey.

• Discuss water safety. Draw and cut out large lifebelt shapes. Decorate with rope patterns. Write some safety rules inside these and display on a water background, or write rescue stories.

• Look at the flags in Dufy's painting. Copy them and try to identify their countries of origin. Draw and colour a variety of flags and use in a boat display.

THE TWO CYCLISTS, MOTHER AND CHILD, 1951
by Fernand Léger (1881–1955)

The Two Cyclists, Mother and Child, 1951, by Fernand Léger (1881–1955) Fondation Beyeler, Riehen/Basel

Fernand Léger came from Normandy in France and trained as an architectural draughtsman. He was inspired by the Machine Age that created such an exciting and hopeful atmosphere in the early twentieth century. He was also interested as an artist in the links between modern themes and traditions of the past, for example mother and child.

When he went to New York, he liked the flashing neon lights and their brilliant colours that illuminated people and things at random. He tried to reproduce this effect by using blocks of colour and drawing freely on top with black lines. The strong straight blocks of colour cut across the simple lines of the picture, providing a bold contrast. As Léger himself wrote, 'The more contrasts there are in a painting, the stronger the work is.'

In the last decade of his life, he liked to observe the working people enjoying themselves in their free-time activities – the circus, cycling, going for picnics, and swimming. The mother and child in this picture are posed almost as in a holiday snapshot. They are wearing sporting clothes designed for cycling.

CELLOPHANE BICYCLES

White paper for background
Small pieces of cellophane in bright colours
Sheets of coloured cellophane larger than the background (this should be a pale colour, for example yellow)
Black wool or string
Scissors and glue

1. Using the cellophane pieces, cut out some shapes, for example triangles, rectangles, squares. Glue them on to the white background leaving spaces between them.
2. Turn the picture over on to the large sheet of cellophane. Glue around the edges on the back of the white paper and fold the surplus cellophane on to the glue. Turn over.
3. Create a picture of a vehicle using black wool glued on to the cellophane. Leave to dry.

• When dry, place the picture under some heavy books to flatten out the cellophane.

• A window version of this could be made using a cardboard frame and gluing the cellophane across this. Add the shapes. Try other media instead of wool, for example strips of black paper or black paint. Attach it to the window.

• Using painted art straws, design a bicycle or other form of transport. It could be glued flat on to a piece of coloured card or glued standing up as a three-dimensional model.

• In pairs, one child draws random coloured shapes with felt-tip pens on a piece of paper. Once completed, pass this to the other child, who can turn it around in any direction and draw a vehicle using a black felt-tip pen over the shapes. Some of the shapes can be coloured in.

• Make a mobile of wheel shapes by gluing a black cardboard ring on to a piece of cellophane. Trim around the outside edge of the ring and draw, paint or add black strips to make a wheel. Hang these one under another against a window.

TRANSPORT PICTURES

Large piece of white paper for background
Pieces of tissue paper in bright colours
Black paper – cut into strips
Scissors and glue

1. Cut the tissue paper into irregular shapes and glue on to the white paper background.
2. Arrange the black paper strips to make a vehicle. Make wheels by cutting rings from black paper and adding strips for spokes.
3. Glue the vehicle on to the tissue-covered background and leave to dry.

WAVY LINE PICTURE

Coloured paper for background
Strips of contrasting paper
Small sheet of white paper
Fine black felt-tip pen
Pencil and eraser
Glue

1. Glue the strips on to the background paper to form stripes.
2. Using a pencil, lightly draw the outline of a boat, a car or some other form of transport on to the white paper.
3. Add simple details.
4. Using a felt-tip pen, draw a wavy line along the pencil outline. Repeat for the details.
5. When dry, rub out the pencil lines.

6. Mount the picture on coloured paper and display on the striped background.

• Younger children will find it easier to make a wavy line with a pencil before using a felt-tip pen.

ALONG THE ROAD
White paper for background
Small shapes of coloured paper, for example red square, green rectangle
Black marker pen
Coloured felt-tip pens
Scissors and glue

1. Glue the coloured shapes on to the white paper, leaving spaces between them.
2. Using the black pen, draw a car or other means of transport. Add other details and make into a scene.
3. Colour in some parts of the picture using felt-tip pens.

THEME SUGGESTIONS – TRANSPORT
- Make a moving picture by gluing the drawing of a cyclist to one end of a strip of stiff card. Cut large slits in a coloured background. Push the strip of card through the slit so that the cyclist appears above it. The cyclist can then be moved across the background. Draw three or more places that the cyclist visits on the background. Write about each place on labels.

- Make a tape recording of an imaginary journey on a bicycle or roller skates. Add sounds of places you are passing (for example railway station – train; airport – plane). Use musical instruments if desired. Other children have a photocopied list of words and tick them off when they identify the place.

- Design a board game with a track on it which has a transport theme. It can be a variation of Snakes and Ladders.

- Invent a fantasy form of transport. Make it out of art straws. Write about what it can do, for example go through mountains, perform rescues and go under water.

- Draw a vehicle with a detailed background with black pen. Photocopy this, and glue on to card. Write a story on the back and make it into a jigsaw. (This can be pieced together using either the picture or the story.)

JACKSON POLLOCK (1912–56)

Jackson Pollock was born in Wyoming, USA, and grew up in Arizona and California. He moved to New York in 1930, to study and paint, but often still wore cowboy clothes and was interested in the 'Wild West'.

His most famous works emphasise spontaneity and the actual process of painting. This was called 'Action Painting' and he was known as 'Jack the Dripper'. He laid his canvas on the floor, walking around it, pouring, dripping and squirting paint with brushes, glass tubes and all sorts of other implements. He said "On the floor, I am more at ease. I feel nearer, more a part of the painting, since this way I can walk around it, work from the four sides and literally be in the painting. This is akin to the method of the Indian sand painters of the west."

His masterpiece, *Blue Poles* (not shown here), was created in this way using oil, enamel and aluminium paint on canvas. It is clear from the distinct layers of paint built up over some time that it was carefully and deliberately painted, but still has the excitement and wildness of spontaneous action.

ACTION PAINTING
Newspaper for experimenting
Coloured paper for background
Brightly coloured liquid paint in squeezy bottles
   (experiment with the consistency)

1. Place newspaper on the floor. Stand over the paper and squeeze the paint gently on to it, using up and down movements (holding the paint bottle upright).

2. After experimenting on newspaper, use the same technique on a plain coloured background. Use three or four colours only. When the picture is completely dry, add white as the final colour. This helps to keep the colours clear and bright.

- Place a long strip of wallpaper on the floor with the plain side up. Find various ways to squirt or drip paint on to this. When dry, use it to cover large areas, for example as backing on display boards, or as a stage backdrop.

- Cover a long rectangle of paper with a layer of strong glue which has had some water added to it. Use different coloured wools to create patterns on the surface. Leave it to dry before moving the picture.

- Place some coloured paper on the floor. Cut out some shapes from cardboard and place these on top of the paper. Drip paint from various implements such as sticks, lids and straws. Carefully lift off the cardboard shapes and see what patterns have been created. Add some more drip patterns over the picture if desired.

SWIRLING

Using a squeezy bottle of liquid glue, make swirling patterns on a dark background (no straight lines). Sprinkle with powder paint in a variety of colours. Shake off the excess. Leave to dry.

- Use old pepper pots or spice containers to sprinkle the powder paint.

- Add glitter if desired.

STRING BLOCK PRINTING

Strong paper or thin card for background	Block of wood
Wool or string	Paint and brushes

1. Wrap wool or string around the block of wood. Wind it to make a pattern and tie it in a knot.
2. Using a brush, paint the wool.
3. Press the block on to the paper. Repeat all over.

- Drip paint on to the background and hold the paper vertically to let the paint run over the surface. When dry, see what patterns have been created. Give the picture a title.

- Print several sheets on different coloured paper. When dry, cut them up and make a landscape picture.

THEME SUGGESTIONS – COLOUR, SHAPE AND PATTERN

- Use one of the techniques to make a picture. Fill in some of the spaces with felt-tip pen. Turn the paper around and write about what you imagine you can see.

- Make a picture using the swirling technique. Write words in the spaces to describe the lines, for example wriggly, circular, curling, twisting.

- Choose one of these ideas to create a weather picture, for example snowy, rainy, stormy, misty, windy. Think about appropriate colours.

THE SNAIL, 1953
by Henri Matisse (1869–1954)

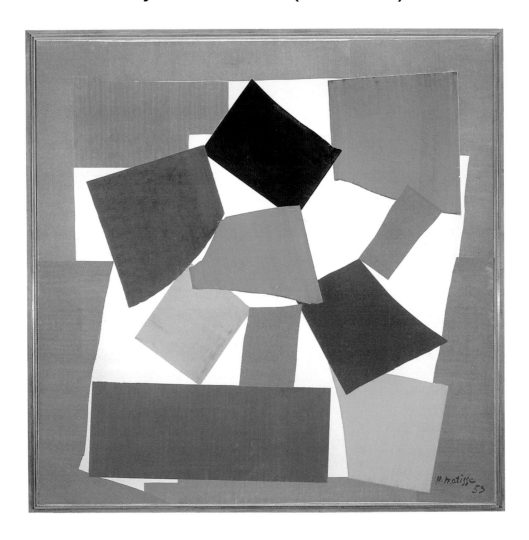

The Snail, **1953, by Henri Matisse (1869–1954), © Tate Gallery, London 1999**
© Succession H. Matisse/DACS 1999

When he created this picture, Matisse was living in the south of France on the Côte d'Azur (the Blue Coast), famous for its beautiful weather, brightly coloured sky and beaches. The colours he has chosen reflect what he saw around him – blue for sea and sky, orange for a hot sunny day, different greens for trees and grass. He used the three primary and the three secondary colours, as well as black and white.

Matisse overlaps the complementary colours (green and red, purple and yellow, orange and blue). The picture is very large (2.8 metres square) and the bright shapes make the spiral seem to vibrate.

Matisse was 84 and could no longer work at an easel. He was crippled with arthritis and confined to bed, but still made wonderful works such as the one above with the help of his assistants. They painted paper with various colours of gouache, and when Matisse had torn or cut them into the shapes he wanted, his assistants pinned them on to the large white background as he directed. Matisse was very exact about the position of each piece. The pin marks can still be seen in the original of the picture shown above. After Matisse had supervised the arrangement, it was then sent to Paris for the shapes to be pasted on to the background. Before this took place, the whole picture was traced over with extreme care to make sure that no changes were made.

The picture above suggests a spiral. Matisse had been drawing many spiral shapes from nature, including snails and shells. There is a tiny silhouette of a snail in purple at the top left-hand corner, which is visible in the original painting.

LOOPED SPIRAL (on the right)
Paper for background
Pastels (same colours as in Matisse's snail picture, if possible)
Torn strips of paper (the same colours as the pastels)
Pencil and glue

1. Draw a large spiral on the background paper with pencil.
2. Start at the centre and fill in with blocks of colour, using the pastels. Keep turning the paper to avoid smudging.
3. Make the torn strips of paper into loops, and glue on to the spiral, where the colours match.

ABSTRACT SPIRAL (on the left)
Look at the colours Matisse has used in his picture. On a circle of card, draw a spiral pattern and colour it with pastels. Cut out shapes from coloured paper and glue down on to the spiral background.

- On a strip of paper, using pastels, draw small blocks of colour. Mix some of these by rubbing with your finger to make other colours.

- Experiment with other ways to make a spiral using pastels and coloured paper.

- Extend this activity by adding colourful bodies to create large fantasy snails.

- Make mobiles using thin card cut into round, square or triangular shapes and then follow the outlines to create spirals. Decorate these with small pieces of shiny paper, cut into the same spiral shape. These make effective dangling Christmas decorations.

- Make a spiral board game with a large round spiral shape drawn with coloured felt-tip pens on coloured card. Write numbers and messages on the track. Make two or more snails from modelling material and race these to the centre of the spiral.

TORN PAPER SPIRAL

Paper for background
Small pieces of paper in the colours of Matisse's snail
Black marker pen
Pencil and glue

1. Draw a large spiral shape in pencil on the background paper, leaving a wide space between the lines.
2. Draw on top of this line with a black marker pen.
3. Spread glue in the central part of the spiral and tear some of the coloured paper into smaller pieces.
4. Place these pieces on the glued background in a sequence to make a repeating pattern. Continue this process to complete the spiral. Leave to dry.
5. Trace over the spiral once more with the black pen.

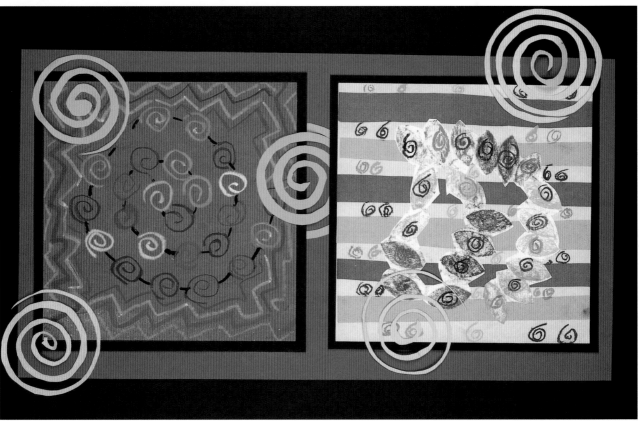

SPIRAL OF SPIRALS

Think of ways to create a 'Spiral of Spirals' picture using coloured paper, pastels and felt-tip pens.
Experiment with drawing ideas first on white paper, then make a coloured version. Try these ideas:

1. Pink background: Using brightly coloured paper, draw small spirals to make a large spiral shape in the centre of the picture. Decorate the background with brightly coloured patterns.
2. Green and yellow background: Make a striped background using brightly coloured paper. Create a spiral on a sheet of white paper using rubbing and drawing techniques. Cut around the spiral shape and glue it on to the striped background.

- The photographs on this page show examples of round spirals. Try drawing triangular, rectangular and square spiral shapes. Make some of these large, using paint and other media, including glitter.
- Using a small piece of card, cut out a spiral shape and rub over it with a wax crayon. Move the shape around to make a large spiral.

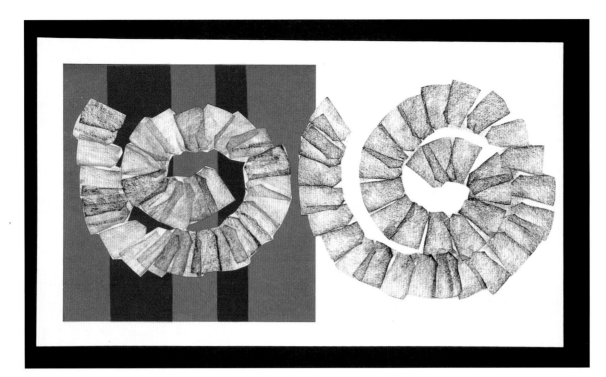

SNAIL RUBBINGS

Coloured paper for background
Strips of coloured paper
Thin white paper for rubbing
Small piece of card
A variety of wax crayons (with wrappers removed)
Scissors and glue

1. Cut a small shape from card.
2. Place this under the centre of the white paper.
3. Using the side of a crayon, rub firmly.
4. Move the shape and repeat to form a spiral of rubbings.
5. Cut out the whole spiral shape.
6. Decorate the background paper with the coloured strips and glue down the spiral.

- Younger children may find it easier to do this rubbing if the shape is fixed to the surface (using a small piece of masking tape). The paper can then be moved around to form a spiral.
- Try using black only, as in the photograph.

THEME SUGGESTIONS – COLOUR, SHAPE AND PATTERN

- Make a book with a circular cover and pages. Draw a spiral on the front and glue a small piece of coloured paper on each page, giving each page one of the colours used in Matisse's painting. Write what each colour makes you think of, for example 'Blue is like the sea or the sky'. Make the writing follow the shape of the circular page.

- Make a picture in pairs. One child with a picture in mind (for example, a simple train) directs the other child to place coloured paper shapes (for example, squares, circles and rectangles) on a background. Try this behind a screen. Glue the shapes down if desired. Check that the picture looks like the one imagined.

- Using the above idea, children record simple instructions on a tape which can then be played to a larger group.

- Find spiral shapes from other countries and cultures, for example Greek and Celtic. Try to discover the significance of these. Look for modern symbols and their meanings.

For details of further Belair publications,
please write to Libby Masters,
BELAIR PUBLICATIONS LIMITED,
Apex Business Centre,
Boscombe Road, Dunstable, LU5 4RL.

For sales and distribution in North America and South America,
INCENTIVE PUBLICATIONS,
3835 Cleghorn Avenue, Nashville, Tn 37215,
USA.

For sales and distribution in Australia,
EDUCATIONAL SUPPLIES PTY LTD,
8 Cross Street, Brookvale, NSW 2100,
Australia.

For sales and distribution (in other territories),
FOLENS PUBLISHERS,
Apex Business Centre,
Boscombe Road, Dunstable, LU5 4RL,
United Kingdom.
Email: folens@folens.com